Sports Are the Best!

BASEBALL IS THE BEST!

by Joe Tischler

PEBBLE
a capstone imprint

Pebble is published by Capstone,
1710 Roe Crest Drive, North Mankato, Minnesota 56003
capstonepub.com

Library of Congress Cataloging-in-Publication Data is available on the Library of Congress website.

ISBN: 9798875256073 (hardcover)
ISBN: 9798875256028 (paperback)
ISBN: 9798875256035 (ebook pdf)

Summary: Easy-to-read text and bright photographs describe the rules, positions, skills, stars, and more of baseball. A short quiz at the end of the book lets the reader test what they've learned.

Editorial Credits
Editor: Erika L. Shores; Designer: Hilary Wacholz; Media Researcher: Svetlana Zhurkin; Production Specialist: Tori Abraham

Image Credits
Getty Images: Brian Fluharty, 15, Chris Coduto, 29, Donald Miralle, cover (left), Duane Burleson, 21, Harry How, 8, Kevork Djansezian, 23, Lorado, 10, Michael Owens, 26, Sarah Stier, 9, Shoji Fujita, cover (right), Stacy Revere, 25, Stephen Brashear, 27; Shutterstock: Andrea Catenaro, 5, Blueberry_80, 18, Cheryl Ann Quigley, 22, Conor P. Fitzgerald, 4, 19, Desmond Adkins, 7, halwani wani (net), throughout, Labunskiy Konstantin (baseball), back cover, 1, 2, 30, Monkey Business Images, 13, PeopleImages.com - Yuri A, cover (middle), 12, pics721, 11, YES Market Media, 16

Printed and bound in China. 006459

Table of Contents

Words in **bold** are in the glossary.

Play Ball!

Hear the crack of the bat. Listen to the pop of the ball in the glove. Smell the great food. You are at a baseball game!

James Outman

Baseball is called America's pastime. People have played the game for nearly 200 years. What is it that makes baseball so great?

Baseball is fun to watch on TV. Watching the best plays on replay is exciting. It is great to attend games in person too. Many stadiums have activities for kids. Baseball fans enjoy stadium food. Hot dogs and pretzels are some of the top foods eaten at games.

Star players help the game of baseball shine. Major League Baseball (MLB) has plenty of standout players. Shohei Ohtani and Aaron Judge are two of them. They hit a lot of **home runs**. Each player has won multiple **Most Valuable Player** (MVP) awards.

Shohei Ohtani

Aaron Judge

What Do You Need to Play?

Baseball is fun because it's a team sport. You can play with friends and family. Boys and girls can play.

Most games are played outdoors. The game is played on a field called a diamond. Four bases are placed around the diamond. Players run to these bases. Behind the diamond is a grassy outfield.

You don't need a lot of equipment to play baseball. You need a ball, a bat, and a glove. Players need to wear helmets for safety when they bat.

Baseball gloves are made of leather. If you throw right-handed, you wear a glove on your left hand. If you throw left-handed, you wear the glove on your right hand. A baseball catcher wears a special glove that is bigger.

Rules of Baseball

It's fun to score in baseball! Points are called **runs**. The team with the most runs at the end of the game wins!

A baseball game is made up of **innings**. An inning is made up of three **outs** for each team. Each team gets a chance to bat. The batting team tries to score runs before the third out is recorded.

FENWAY PARK
P 1 2 3 4 5 6 7 8 9 10
16 CHICAGO 0 0 0 0 0 0 0 0
71 BOSTON 2 0 0 1 6 0 2 6
BALL
STRIKE
OUT
H
CHICAGO
4

To score a run, a batter needs to touch all the bases. A batter starts at home plate. The batter tries to hit the pitched ball. If the batter swings and misses, it is a strike. A strike also happens if a batter does not swing at a good pitch. Three strikes is an out.

A pitcher might throw a bad pitch. It is called a ball. Four balls is a walk. Then the batter goes to first base. It is the next batter's turn.

Baseball Positions

To keep the batting team from scoring, the other team plays positions in the field. Four of the players are called infielders. They play near the bases.

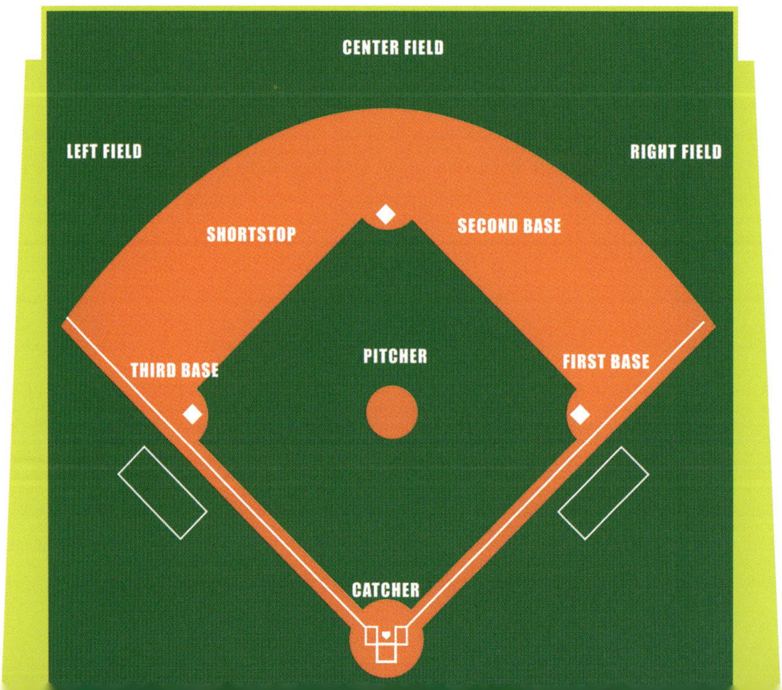

A first baseman catches the ball for an out.

Infield positions are called first base, second base, third base, and shortstop. If a ball is hit on the ground to these positions, the player throws the ball to the nearest base. The player who catches the ball tags the batter or steps on the base first for an out.

Outfielders stand in the grass behind the infielders. Outfield positions are left field, center field, and right field.

Batters might hit balls past the infielders. The outfielders then run to get the ball. They throw it to an infielder. An outfielder might catch a hit ball in the air. That's an out.

Manuel Margot

A catcher receives the pitch from the pitcher. The pitcher stands on a mound in the middle of the diamond. The catcher is behind home plate.

The pitcher throws different types of pitches. The pitcher and catcher work together to decide on what pitch to throw. They try to get the batter out with strikes.

Baseball Skills

As a baseball player, you have many ways to help your team win. The best pro players are known as "five-tool" players. They are great at five important skills.

The first two tools involve batting. Good hand-eye **coordination** gets you on base more. The more you can connect the pitch to your swing of the bat, the more hits you will get. The next skill involves power. Can you swing and hit the ball hard?

Aaron Judge

Mike Trout

Speed is the third tool. After you hit the ball, how fast can you run? Fast players get around the bases and score.

Speed is good for playing positions. The faster you can get to the ball, the more outs you can get. This goes with the fourth tool, fielding. Can you catch or grab the ball? That leads into the final tool, arm strength. Can you throw the ball far? A player with a strong arm is good in the outfield.

Seiya Suzuki

Is Baseball the Best?

Baseball is a sport you can enjoy with your friends and family. Summer days in the park are great with a bat, a ball, and a glove.

You can bring your glove to watch your favorite team in person. Catching a ball hit into the stands is a thrill. You get to keep the ball!

What do you like best about baseball?

Test Your Baseball Knowledge

Now that you've read this book, are you a baseball expert? Take this quiz to find out! If you don't know the answer, read the book again, and you might be able to find it.

1. On which hand does a right-handed player wear a baseball glove?

   a. Right hand

   b. Left hand

   c. Either hand

2. How many players are in the outfield?

   a. 2

   b. 3

   c. 4

3. How many strikes is an out?

   a. 1

   b. 2

   c. 3

Answers: 1b; 2b; 3c

Glossary

coordination (koh-OR-duh-nay-shun)—able to control body movements

home run (HOHM RUN)—a hit in baseball that allows the batter to go completely around the bases and score a run

inning (IN-ing)—one part of a baseball game, each team gets a chance to bat and try to score; most baseball games have nine innings

Most Valuable Player (MVP) (MOST VAL-yoo-buhl PLAY-ur)—an award given to the year's best player

out (OWT)—when a base runner must leave the field because they weren't able to reach the base before the ball; three strikes is also an out

run (RUHN)—in baseball, a player crosses home plate to score

Index

About the Author

Joe Tischler is an author and sportswriter who lives in southern Minnesota. When he's not writing about sports, he's watching sports. As a lifelong Minnesotan, he is an avid fan of Minnesota sports teams including the Vikings, Twins, Timberwolves, and Golden Gophers. He's happily married to Gwen and is a proud father to son Toby.